First published in Great Britain in 2008 by Buster Books,
an imprint of Michael O'Mara Books Limited,
9 Lion Yard, Tremadoc Road, London SW4 7NQ

Written by Helen Stradling
Illustrated by Katy Jackson
Created and produced by The Complete Works
St Mary's Road, Royal Leamington Spa, Warwickshire CV31 1JP
Produced by Joanne Rooke
Cover by Zoe Quayle (from a design by www.blacksheep-uk.com)
Cover illustration by Paul MoranProduced by Joanne Rooke
A CIP catalogue record for this book is available from the British Library

ISBN: 978-1-906082-34-5

2 4 6 8 10 9 7 5 3 1

www.mombooks.com/busterbooks

Printed and bound in Italy by Rotolito Lombarda

Papers used by Buster Books are natural, recyclable products made from wood grown in sustainable forests. The manufacturing processes conform to the environmental regulations of the country of origin.

Buster Books

# Contents

# It's A Girls' World

Girls are cool and that's official.
They can dress how they like, think what they
want and achieve anything they dream of.
It's time to celebrate being a girl and that's what
this book is all about. It is written just for you.
You will find fun features, sports tips, quizzes, health and beauty
advice, magical make-overs and loads of great things to make.
Dive into The Girls' Annual and you will find everything
you need to be a seriously cool girl…
and lots more besides.
See ya!

So let the fun begin.
On the page opposite there is a
quiz that will test how much you
know about your sisters around the
world. You will find all the answers
on page 60.

# WHERE IN THE WORLD?

In different countries girls and their families have their own traditional ways of celebrating special occasions. Try this quick quiz to find out more about what your sisters around the world are up to.

**1.** In which country is a birthday girl painted on the forehead with a small mark for good luck, using a mixture of rice, yogurt and dye?
**a)** Denmark **b)** Iceland **c)** Nepal.

**2.** In which country does a girl receive a pull on the earlobe on her birthday for every year she has lived?
**a)** Argentina **b)** Austria **c)** Brazil.

**3.** In which country could a girl be given a birthday pie with a message in the pastry, instead of a cake?
**a)** Australia **b)** New Zealand **c)** Russia.

**4.** Where would friends or family give girls a small red packet full of money on their birthday?
**a)** China **b)** Portugal **c)** Norway.

**5.** Where does a girl usually have two birthday parties – one to celebrate her birthday and one on the day of the saint she was named after?
**a)** Congo **b)** Mexico **c)** Tunisia.

**6.** In which country do girls have their nose greased with butter or margarine on their birthday, for good luck?
**a)** Canada **b)** Iran **c)** Ireland.

**7.** Which country celebrates Dolls' Festival or Girls' Day on March 3rd to thank girls for their health and happiness?
**a)** Ireland **b)** Japan **c)** South Africa.

**8.** In which country do children leave shoes out for the good Christmas Witch, La Befana, to fill with all kinds of presents on Christmas Eve?
**a)** Italy **b)** Romania **c)** Switzerland.

**9.** Where do girls wear this traditional costume – a white blouse, a black and white skirt, a red flannel shawl, a white apron, black stockings and shoes and a tall black hat?
**a)** Nepal **b)** Spain **c)** Wales.

**10.** In which country would a birthday girl be served extra-long noodles for lunch to symbolise an extra-long life?
**a)** Germany **b)** Ghana **c)** USA.

**11.** In which country might you see young girls carrying lighted candles and flowers to the cemetery on the 'Day of the Dead', while their brothers and fathers watch them from a distance?
**a)** Australia **b)** Mexico **c)** Sweden.

# Choc-tastic!

*It's made from the beans of a tree and the ancient Aztecs and Mayas worshipped it. It is one of the most popular flavours in the world, and girls love to eat it. What is it? Chocolate, of course! Here are some yummy recipes for you to try.*

## CHOCOLATE BISCOTTI

Biscotti are crisp Italian biscuits and are great to dunk in a mug of hot chocolate. Impress your friends by baking some today.

**You will need:**
100 g plain flour /
120 g caster sugar /
50 g cocoa powder /
½ tsp baking powder /
1 tsp orange essence or
½ tsp almond essence /
½ tsp salt / 2 eggs.

1. First, preheat an oven to 180°C/Gas Mark 4.
2. Then, in a bowl, sift together the flour, sugar, cocoa, salt and baking powder.

3. Whisk the essence into the eggs in another bowl.
4. Stir this into the flour mixture until you have a soft, sticky ball of dough. The mixture won't spread properly if it is too stiff, so add a dash of water if you need to.

5. Stop the dough sticking to your fingers by sprinkling some flour on to your hands. Then place the dough onto a greased baking tray and shape into a log, about 35 centimetres long and 5 centimetres wide. Put the tray into the oven and bake for 25 minutes.

6. When ready, remove the baking tray and turn the log out onto a wire rack to cool. Now turn the oven down to 150°C/Gas Mark 2.

7. Cut the log diagonally into slices 1.5 centimetres thick. Place the slices back on the baking tray on their sides and put them back in the oven for between 15 and 20 minutes. Remember to turn them all over onto their other side half way through.
8. Finally, remove them and leave them on a wire rack to cool.

## • SAFETY WARNING •

• Don't risk burning your fingers – always ask an adult to help each time you use the oven.
• Always use oven gloves when handling hot baking trays.

# PARTY BROWNIES

These brownies are not very healthy, but they make a great treat, so why not have a go?

## You will need:
150 g plain chocolate /
120 g unsalted butter /
2 large eggs, beaten /
250 g caster sugar / 30 g cocoa powder / 75 g plain flour /
½ tsp baking powder /
75 g mini marshmallows.

1. Preheat an oven to 190°C/Gas Mark 5.
2. Take a 30 by 20 centimetre baking tin, line it with greaseproof paper and grease with some butter.

3. Melt the chocolate and butter in a bowl sitting over a pan of simmering water. Stir constantly.

When melted, take the pan off the heat and leave to cool for a few minutes.

4. Beat the eggs and sugar together with a wooden spoon in a bowl until creamy. Sift the flour, cocoa powder and baking powder and fold the mixture together.

5. When the mixture is completely smooth, pour the melted chocolate and butter into the bowl and stir in thoroughly. Finally add in the marshmallows.

6. Put the brownie mixture into the baking tin and spread it out to the edges. Bake for around 25 minutes, until the surface has set, but it still feels soft underneath – get an adult to test this for you. Leave the brownies to cool completely, then slice and eat.

# CHOCOLATE COMFORT

This hot drink is delicious, especially when it's chilly outside. Why not make it for somebody special to enjoy?

## You will need for one cup:
a cup or mug
of milk / a small bar
of dark chocolate /
chocolate flavoured
dessert topping syrup /
whipped cream –
fresh or in a spray can.

1. Pour the milk into a saucepan to warm, then pour into a mug.

2. Crumble the chocolate bar into the milk and stir it in as it melts.
3. Squirt the chocolate flavoured dessert syrup on top and add a big dollop of whipped cream. Gorgeous!

# Let's Jump!

*You may think that skipping is old-fashioned, but it's actually a really good way to keep fit. Some of the world's top athletes and dancers use it in their work-out routines so, have a go.*

## THE BASICS

Before you try the more difficult jumps, make sure you warm up with some basic ones – try ten of each.

### BASIC JUMP
Turn the rope and jump as it touches the ground.

### DOUBLE JUMP
Make a bigger jump and turn the rope twice under your feet before you land.

### HOP AND SKIP
Land on your left foot, then swap to your right.

### JUMPING JILL
Land with your feet apart and then together, as you jump.

### CROSS-OVER
Cross your arms in front of you as you jump over the rope.

## JUMP ROUTINE ONE
Start with some basic jumps to build up a rhythm, then work through the five basic moves – doing five of each.

## • TOP TIPS •
• Stand up tall, but keep relaxed and skip on your tiptoes.
• Swing the rope by rotating your wrists, and try not to wave your arms around too much.
• While turning the rope, keep your elbows low and tucked into your sides.
• Don't skip too slowly, because the rope might get caught by your feet.
• Bend your knees a little as you land, to reduce the 'jolt' of the jump.
• Jump just high enough for the rope to pass under your feet.
• Good breathing technique can improve your stamina, so practise breathing in for two seconds and out for two, then in for three and out for three.

Now it's time for some more difficult moves.

## SKIP SLALOM

This one is like skiing a slalom because you twist your knees to the left and then the right as you land.

## FIGURE-OF-EIGHT

This time there's no need to jump. Keep your hands together and sweep the rope in a figure-of-eight pattern through the air – first to the left of your body and then to the right.

## KICK AND SKIP

This one's a bit like dancing the can-can. As you turn the rope, keep your knees slightly bent and land on alternate feet. When you land on your right foot, raise your left leg and when you land on your left foot, raise your right.

## BACKWARD JUMP

Do a basic jump, but turn the rope the other way.

## BALANCED JUMP

This one's quite tricky. Turn the rope forward and put your right hand under your right knee. Carry on skipping, landing on your left leg. Then put your left hand under your left knee and keep going landing on your right leg this time.

# JUMP ROUTINE TWO

Once you've mastered all the moves, have a go at routine two to test your skipping skills. It combines some of the basic moves with some of the more difficult ones. If you've got a group of friends who can all skip, why not try doing the routine together, in time with some music?

10 jumping jills / 9 backward jumps
8 skip slaloms / 7 figures-of-eight
6 cross-overs / 5 kick and skips
4 basic jumps / 3 hop and skips
2 double jumps / 1 balanced jump.

Now try making up some of your own jumps and put them together in a new routine. A good tip is to save your most difficult move until the end, for an impressive finale.

# Secret Diaries

*A diary is more than just a list of the things you've done. It can be like a special friend you can confide in and it's a great way to wind down after a busy day. So, why not follow these simple instructions and make one of your own?*

## DENIM DIARY

Try making this cool diary with a hint of retro chic. Denim is a great material to use because it's hard wearing, but easy to use and it's always in fashion.

**You will need:** a small hardback notebook / tissue paper or newspaper / a pencil / scissors / pins / denim material – an old pair of jeans will do nicely / fabric or PVA glue / needle and thread / small hair bobble / a large button or bead / coloured card.

1. First, create a template. Open the notebook out flat and place on the tissue paper or newspaper. Leave a space at least two-fingers wide around the edge and draw around it. Cut the shape out carefully with scissors.

2. Pin your paper template to the denim and cut the shape out from the material.

3. Keeping the notebook out flat, turn it so the cover faces upwards and smear the front and back covers with a lot of glue.

4. Place the denim on top and press firmly. To get it really smooth, try hanging the opened diary over a table edge and smooth the fabric over the front and then the back. This allows for some 'give' in the material, so the diary will close properly once the material is stuck. Before you press the material down firmly, close the diary and open it up again and make any little adjustments to the denim.

5. Trim around the edges of the denim to leave a slight overhang, about a centimetre wide.

6. Open the book and fold the overhang around the inside edges of the cover and stick down with glue. If you cut the material at the corners, as shown, it will make it easier to fold neatly. Tuck any excess fabric into the spine of the notebook.

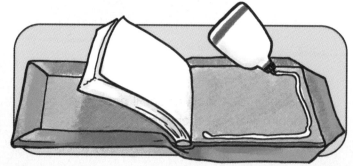

**7.** Quickly, before the glue dries, use the needle and thread to stitch the hair bobble to the back cover.

**8.** Stretch the bobble round to the front of the diary, but don't pull it too tight. Draw a dot with a pencil to mark where it reaches. Stitch on the button or bead over the dot to make a fastening.

**9.** Cut out two pieces of card, each a little bit smaller than the notebook's cover. Glue one to the inside front cover and one to the inside back cover to secure the fabric more firmly and to hide any rough edges.

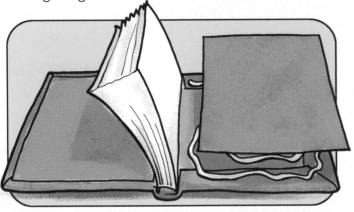

## • TOP TIP •

If there's a belt loop, or small pocket in your denim material, then why not use it as a handy place to keep a pen?

# PADDED DIARY

Padded or quilted covers give a really cool look to a diary and you don't need to be a professional designer to make yourself one.

**You will need:** scissors / thick card / a spiral-bound notebook / fabric or PVA glue / a sheet of wadding or foam / fabric that you can't see through / newspaper / ribbon.

**1.** Cut out two pieces of card, the same size as the front cover of your notebook.

**2.** Dilute some glue with an equal amount of water, then cover one piece of card with it and stick on the foam or wadding. If some of the foam or wadding is hanging over the edges of the card then trim this off. Now do the same with the other piece of card.

**3.** Next cut out two pieces of fabric, each about two-fingers' width larger than the size of the card. (It might be easier to make a paper template you can cut around first – see Denim Diary.)

**4.** Place one piece of fabric onto some newspaper and cover the reverse of it with glue. Then place the padded side of one of the card pieces in the centre of the fabric. Press firmly down to make it stick, adding more glue if necessary. Once it sticks, do the same with the other piece of card.

**5.** Cut the material at the corners, as shown, and fold the overhanging fabric over and stick to the back of the cards with more glue.

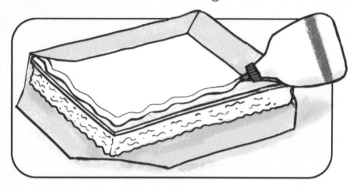

**6.** Open your notebook and lay it out flat, with the cover facing up. Cover just the front with glue and place the ribbon across it so some hangs over the edge. This will be used to tie the diary shut.

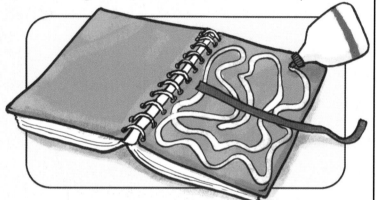

**7.** Now stick one of the pieces of quilted card onto the glue, over the ribbon and press it down firmly.

**8.** Do the same thing with the back cover – don't forget to add another length of ribbon with some hanging over the edge.

**9.** Put some heavy objects, such as books, on top of the open diary overnight, to allow the glue to set. Now it is time to start writing your diary.

## • TOP TIP •

Give your diary some sparkle by sticking colourful beads and sequins to the cover with dabs of glue.

# I DIDN'T KNOW THAT!

Anne Frank (1929–1945) was a young Jewish girl who kept a diary during the Second World War. While she and her family hid from the Nazis, Anne wrote about the horrors of war, as well as the everyday problems of being a teenager. Published as 'The Diary of Anne Frank', it has been translated into 50 different languages and is one of the most read books in the world.

# Premiere Drama

Jessica, Sunee and Alana squealed excitedly as a pink stretch limousine pulled up outside and tooted. A tall, young woman stepped out and waved. 'Hello, girls. I'm Milli and here are your VIP tickets.'

The girls ran towards the limo where Milli gave them their tickets.

Congratulations!
As winners of the 'Biggest Fan' competition, you are invited to the premiere of the new movie 'Sensational!' starring pop divas *Rose Bouquet.*
Join the pop trio in the royal box at the glitzy Ritz Cinema and afterwards for a special performance at the Ritz Ballroom.

The girls giggled with glee and jumped into the car.

An hour later, just as it was getting dark, they spotted the Ritz Cinema with hundreds of *Rose Bouquet* fans and photographers eagerly waiting – everyone jostling for the best view. The cinema was covered in sparkling pink lights and the noise was immense.

'*Rose Bouquet* loved the covers of their songs you sent,' said Milli. 'You sounded amazing. Now, it can get pretty mad out there, so we've found you a spot by the entrance where you can wait for *Rose Bouquet* to arrive. I'll see you at the party afterwards.'

The limo slowed down and stopped at the end of a long, pink carpet. Jessica grabbed her friends' hands. 'Come on girls, smile!' she said and stepped out. The photographers went wild and the air was filled with bright lights, as a thousand flashes went off all around.

Then the girls waited by the entrance, as shiny limos kept arriving, full of famous pop and movie stars – the girls were seriously star-struck!

Suddenly, a huge floodlight was switched on. It picked out a bright pink camper van arriving. The van pulled up beside the pink carpet and the side door slid open. And there they were – the three members of *Rose Bouquet.* The girl band, all dressed in sparkly outfits, jumped out. 'We're here,' they cried together.

The crowd went berserk! 'TARA! JADE! ELLIE!' they screamed. The girls waved to their adoring fans. Then Milli whispered in Jade's ear and the girl band headed straight towards Jessica, Sunee and Alana.

'Hello,' said Jade to the girls. 'Come on. You're with us!' They ducked under the security rope and were soon walking arm-in-arm with the stars.

'Let's find our seats,' shouted Ellie over the noise. 'My feet are killing me in these boots.'

Minutes later, all six had been ushered into the royal box. Then the lights dimmed and the film premiere started. Milli popped in with a big box of chocolates.

Tara passed the chocolates round. 'White truffles,' she whispered to Sunee. 'My faves!'

It wasn't long before Ellie started fidgeting. 'Listen girls,' she said. 'These boots are pinching me like crazy. I'm going to run back to the dressing room upstairs and change into my trainers.'

'Be quick,' whispered Tara. 'It's not long 'till our performance.'

But ten minutes later Ellie hadn't returned.

'I wonder where she is,' said Jade. 'Someone should go and check that she's okay.'

'People will notice if you disappear, too, so we'll go,' offered Jessica. 'Won't we, girls?' Her friends nodded eagerly and the three quietly slipped out of the royal box into the corridor outside.

'Look,' said Jessica. 'Stairs. Ellie said that she had to go upstairs to change her boots. So let's go.'

At the top of the stairs was a door. Suddenly, they heard a groan. Sunee put her finger to her lips to tell the others to be quiet, and slowly opened the door.

And there was Ellie, propped up against a wall with one leg sticking out awkwardly. She looked upset and her face was quite pale. In one hand was the broken heel of her boot and in the other was her mobile.

'What happened?' asked Alana, rushing to her side. 'Do you want us to get a doctor?'

'No thanks,' said Ellie, 'I've just sprained my ankle. I came in here and saw three guys trying to steal our costumes, so I got my mobile out and they ran off down the corridor towards the dressing room. I tried to follow and that's when the heel of my boot snapped off and I fell down.'

Suddenly the girls heard footsteps and talking. 'They are coming back,' said Ellie. 'Quickly, we must hide.'

Sunee and Jessica hauled the pop star to her feet, while Alana frantically started opening doors.

She soon found a small cupboard, just big enough for all the girls to hide in. Sunee and Jessica grabbed Ellie and piled in, pulling the door shut behind them just in time. They all held their breath.

'Looks like that girl has gone,' they heard a man say. 'Come on, we don't have much time. Let's get back to the dressing room and steal what we can and go.'

The voices faded and the girls breathed a sigh of relief.

Then Jessica had an idea. 'I'll be back in a sec,' she said. She grabbed a broom and tiptoed towards the dressing room where the men were. Without a second thought, she slammed the door to the room shut, and wedged the broom handle against the door, trapping the thieves inside. 'That should hold them,' she muttered. There were angry shouts from inside the dressing room and the door rattled, but the broom held it closed.

'Great!' said Ellie. 'I'll phone the police on my mobile.'

Minutes later, Jessica, Sunee, Alana and Ellie were back on the pink carpet, as two police cars raced up and six police officers piled into the building. 'We'll take it from here,' said a policeman to the girls.

'Look,' said Alana, pointing to three people on the roof. 'It's the thieves – they must have gone out of the dressing room's window.'

Jessica spotted the floodlight used earlier for the arrival of *Rose Bouquet*. She switched it on, tilted it up and scanned the rooftop. 'There they are!' she cried, as three figures were caught in the bright glare.

A policewoman radioed her colleagues inside. Just then, there was a bang, as the officers emerged on to the roof. They closed in on the villains, who were quickly overpowered, handcuffed and marched off.

At that moment, the film inside the cinema finished and hundreds of fans poured out, laughing and smiling, ready to go upstairs to the party in the ballroom. 'Ellie!' cried Milli. 'What happened to your ankle?'

Ellie grimaced. 'It's swollen. I don't think I can manage the show. But I have an idea. Girls, are you up for it?'

Jessica, Sunee and Alana were rushed upstairs to the dressing room where a lady appeared with an armful of tops, glittery skirts and sparkling shoes.

Jessica, Sunee and Alana stood in their new clothes in front of the mirror. They looked at each other and screamed with pure delight.

'Wow!' said Ellie. 'Let's just quickly run through the show – I know you know the words and the dance routines already. After all, you are our biggest fans!'

Before long, the three friends were up on the ballroom stage, alongside Tara and Jade, while Ellie watched from the wings. Then the lights turned on and the music started and they were off – singing and dancing on stage with their pop idols.

'We love you!' cried the crowd. 'More! More!'

'Great work,' cried Milli, as the performance finally came to an end. 'You should form your own band.'

Just then, a bouquet landed on the stage in front of them – a bunch of baby pink roses. Sunee picked them up, winked at her friends and smiled. 'And I have the perfect name for us,' she said. '*Rosebudz!*'

# Catwalk Capers

*Welcome to the whirlwind world of high fashion! The cameras are at the ready and the lights are on. Can you complete the puzzles below and become a true fashion babe? All the answers can be found on page 60.*

## ON YOUR TOES

Take a look at the shoes and boots on this rack. How many pairs are there?

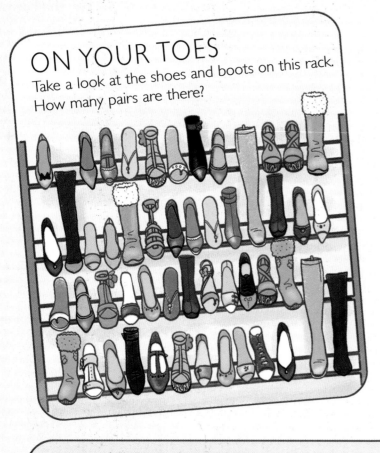

## MAKE-UP FIX

A make-up artist has asked you to arrange her make-up. Every row, every column and each of the four different coloured squares must contain a nail polish (N), a powder compact (C), a lipstick (L) and an eyeliner pencil (E). Can you help by writing in the letters in the correct squares?

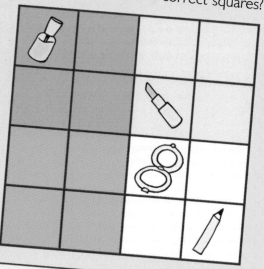

## ALL TANGLED UP

Help these supermodels to deal with their hair. Follow the lines to work out which hair product belongs to which model.

# PHOTO MANIA

Can you work out which photographer took which of the photos at the bottom of the page. You need to consider where each one is standing or sitting and which model they are aiming their camera at.

# Time To Relax

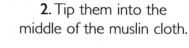

*We all need a bit of pampering sometimes, and warm baths are a great way to relax and unwind. But don't splash out on expensive bath products – make some of your own.*

## SWEET DREAMS

You can make your very own bubble bath mixture by following this simple recipe.

**You will need:** a handful of fresh or dried rose petals / a handful of dried lavender flowers / a square of muslin / some thick thread.

1. Mix all the petals and flowers together in a bowl.

2. Tip them into the middle of the muslin cloth.

3. Pull the corners of the muslin together and tie with the thread. Make a loop to hang it from a tap.

4. Run yourself a warm bath and dangle the bundle in the water.

5. Simply wait for the petals to release their soothing fragrance, then relaaaax.

## SIZZLING BATH SALTS

This herbal recipe will add some zing to your bath time.

**You will need:** 100 g bicarbonate of soda / 50 g citric acid powder (from a chemist or craft shop) / 50 g lightly ground sea salt / 1 tsp of dried rosemary leaves (fresh leaves if you have them).

1. Pour the bicarbonate of soda into a dry bowl and break up any lumps.
2. Add the citric acid powder, sea salt, rosemary and mix together.

3. Store the mixture in a clean, dry jar. Use a heaped tablespoon per bath. Watch as it starts to fizz!

# FIZZY BOMBS

These release all the moisturising goodness of sweet almond oil as they come into contact with hot water. Makes 8 bombs.

**You will need:**
120 g citric acid powder /
350 g bicarbonate of soda /
10 ml (2 tsps) sweet almond oil /
bun tin and paper cases.

1. Sift together the citric acid powder and bicarbonate of soda into a big bowl.

2. Add the almond oil, a few drops at a time, to the mix. Rub it into the powder with your fingertips.

3. Pop 8 paper cases into the tin and spoon the mixture into them. Press down firmly with a metal spoon and leave to set over night.

4. Turn the fizzy bombs out onto a dry tea towel and carefully remove the paper cases. Leave them to dry.

5. Wrap the fizzy bombs in coloured tissue paper and ribbon and put them into a pretty box for a great gift idea.

# IT'S A GIFT

Everyone loves getting homemade toiletries.
* Keep pretty bottles to put some bubble bath in.
* Add some glamour by decorating the bottles with bows, shiny ribbon, or glitter.
* Try placing pretty seashells, or small marbles into the bottom of the bottle.
* Make your gift really special by adding a matching bath puff or sponge.

# Chinese Astrology

*Early Chinese astrologists believed that the date and time of your birth could tell them a lot about your destiny. Read on to find out about your animal sign and the 'inner' and 'secret' you.*

## WHAT'S YOUR SIGN?

While Western astrology is based on the months of the year, Chinese Astrology has a 12-year lunar cycle, starting in January or February each year. It is made up of 12 animal signs and five natural elements, which combine to form the cycle.

Everyone has a Chinese sign and you can find yours by the year you were born in. So, if your birthday is between January 28th, 1998 and February 15th, 1999, you were born in the year of the Tiger. Check out this chart to see which sign you are.

| ELEMENT | ANIMAL | DATE OF BIRTH |
| --- | --- | --- |
| Metal | Horse | Jan 27th, 1990 – Feb 14th, 1991 |
| Metal | Sheep | Feb 15th, 1991 – Feb 3rd, 1992 |
| Water | Monkey | Feb 4th, 1992 – Jan 22nd, 1993 |
| Water | Rooster | Jan 23rd, 1993 – Feb 9th, 1994 |
| Wood | Dog | Feb 10th, 1994 – Jan 30th, 1995 |
| Wood | Pig | Jan 31st, 1995 – Feb 18th, 1996 |
| Fire | Rat | Feb 19th, 1996 – Feb 6th, 1997 |
| Fire | Ox | Feb 7th, 1997 – Jan 27th, 1998 |
| Earth | Tiger | Jan 28th, 1998 – Feb 15th, 1999 |
| Earth | Rabbit | Feb 16th, 1999 – Feb 4th, 2000 |
| Metal | Dragon | Feb 5th, 2000 – Jan 23rd, 2001 |
| Metal | Snake | Jan 24th, 2001 – Feb 11th, 2002 |
| Water | Horse | Feb 12th, 2002 – Jan 31st, 2003 |
| Water | Sheep | Feb 1st, 2003 – Jan 21st, 2004 |
| Wood | Monkey | Jan 22nd, 2004 – Feb 8th, 2005 |

## RATS

People born in the year of the Rat are intelligent, honest, charming and imaginative. They have a good sense of humour and will be very protective and generous to those who are loyal to them.

## OX

If you were born in the year of the Ox you are powerful and kind-hearted. You are a born leader, hard-working and reliable, but you are also affectionate and tender. You enjoy spending time with your friends and they admire the honest advice you give them.

## TIGERS

People born in the year of the Tiger are loyal, wise and daring. They have an air of authority that others are drawn to. They are fun and charming with an exciting, generous personality. They are also sincere and affectionate and care deeply about their friends.

## RABBITS

If you were born in the year of the Rabbit, you are probably quite shy and try to avoid getting into arguments. You are popular with your friends and show them lots of compassion. You are also sensitive and protective of the people you care about.

## DRAGONS

People born in the year of the Dragon are successful and love being the centre of attention. They are powerful and lucky with money. They are also warm-hearted and usually give really good advice.

## SNAKES

If you were born in the year of the Snake you are sociable and well-liked, but you may also feel quite shy sometimes. You are generous and hard-working, and expect the same from your friends. You trust your own judgement.

## HORSES

People born in the year of the Horse are free-spirited and independent. Their freedom is very important to them. They will be loyal and cheerful friends and they have a good sense of humour. Most of all they love to show off!

## SHEEP

If you were born in the year of the Sheep you have a creative, imaginative spirit and you probably spend lots of time day-dreaming. You often worry about things, so you need lots of friends around you who you can trust. You are gentle, honest and peaceful and you always try to see the best in people.

## MONKEYS

People born in the year of the Monkey are lively, fun and full of wit and charm. They like to have a good time and they love being the centre of attention. They are sociable and entertaining, but they also have a wise and sensitive side and they make good listeners.

## ROOSTERS

If you were born in the year of the Rooster you will be quick-thinking and always want to know exactly what's going on. Roosters make great friends because they are truthful and they keep to their word. They are also neat and tidy and they will be generous and loyal to their friends and family.

## DOGS

If you were born in the year of the Dog you are loyal and understanding and you like to do things properly. You make a faithful friend and a good listener, but sometimes you can be quite moody. You are well behaved and responsible and you like helping other people.

## PIGS

If you were born in the year of the Pig you will have good manners and taste and people enjoy hanging out with you. You care deeply about your friends and are generous and sympathetic towards them. You are easy-going and enjoy having the good things in life.

## THE INNER YOU

You might seem like a Dragon or a Tiger on the outside, but there's far more to your personality than that.

In Chinese astrology you have an 'inner' animal and a 'secret' animal, too, depending on the month and hour that you were born.

Your birth year shows us the 'outer' you that people see. The animal of your birth month determines the 'inner' you, which is the person you wish you could be. The animal sign for the hour you were born reveals the 'secret' you. This is the person you really are inside, but the one you stop the rest of the world from seeing.

Look at the chart below to see which inner animal you are. It's all about who you want to be and what you want to do. It tells you about your inner feelings and how you relate to other people.

| DATE | ANIMAL |
| --- | --- |
| Feb 4th – Mar 5th | Tiger |
| Mar 6th – Apr 4th | Rabbit |
| Apr 5th – May 4th | Dragon |
| May 5th – June 5th | Snake |
| June 6th – July 6th | Horse |
| July 7th – Aug 6th | Sheep |
| Aug 7th – Sept 7th | Monkey |
| Sept 8th – Oct 7th | Rooster |
| Oct 8th – Nov 6th | Dog |
| Nov 7th – Dec 6th | Pig |
| Dec 7th – Jan 5th | Rat |
| Jan 6th – Feb 3rd | Ox |

## THE SECRET YOU

Your 'secret' animal sign is believed to reveal your truest self. It is very specific because it is based on the hour you were born, rather than the month, or year.

| TIME | ANIMAL |
| --- | --- |
| 23.00 – 01.00 | Rat |
| 01.00 – 03.00 | Ox |
| 03.00 – 05.00 | Tiger |
| 05.00 – 07.00 | Rabbit |
| 07.00 – 09.00 | Dragon |
| 09.00 – 11.00 | Snake |
| 11.00 – 13.00 | Horse |
| 13.00 – 15.00 | Sheep |
| 15.00 – 17.00 | Monkey |
| 17.00 – 19.00 | Rooster |
| 19.00 – 21.00 | Dog |
| 21.00 – 23.00 | Pig |

# I DIDN'T KNOW THAT!

Chinese astrology is an ancient tradition that has been studied for thousands of years – though the actual date it began is not known. It is older than our zodiac. Millions of people worldwide consult it every day.

# Ocean Centre

*How about a trip to see the creatures at the bottom of the ocean, but without getting wet?*
*Have a go at these puzzles and go to page 60 to discover all the answers.*

## SPOT THE SEAHORSE
How many seahorses can you see in this tank?

## SEEING DOUBLE
Only two of these angelfish are identical, but which two?

A B C D
E F G
H I J

## WHICH WAY IS HOME?
This hermit crab wants to get back to his shell. Can you show him the way?

# DOLPHIN DILEMMA
Can you spot five differences between the two pairs of bottle-nose dolphins?

# SEABED SEARCH
How many starfish and how many sea urchins can you spot?

# TURTLE MIX
Which four of the details below are from the turtle tank picture above?

A  B  C
D  E  F
G  H  I

# Flutterby Butterfly

*Why not show off your artistic skills to somebody special by making a 3-D card for them?*
*It's also great for all kinds of occasions, like a friend's birthday, or Mother's Day.*

**You will need:** a pencil / coloured card / paper / scissors / felt-tip pens.

Below is a template for your flutterby butterfly card. It is based on a square with sides at least 8 centimetres long. The square shape forms the base of the card. The four semi-circles are where you will make the folds, along the dotted lines. The other details will make up the butterfly itself – two antennae at the top, big wings to the left and right and two smaller wings beneath them.

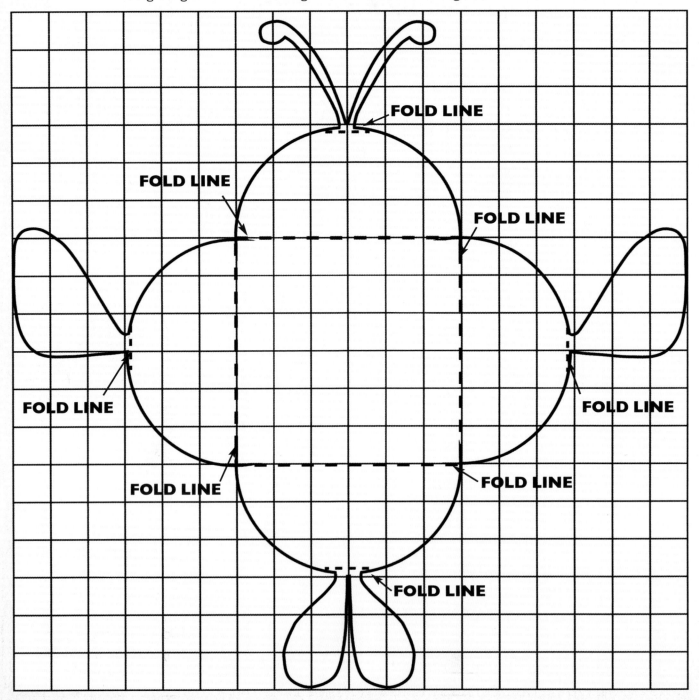

1. Trace the template on page 30 onto a sheet of paper (including the fold lines) and cut it out. To make your card twice as big, use the squares of the grid as a guide to doubling the lengths of each of the lines – this will keep the template of your card in the correct proportions for folding.

2. Choose your favourite colour of card – green works well. Place the template on it and draw around it carefully and add in the fold lines.

3. Cut out the shape and fold it along the square fold lines, as shown.

4. Then fold out the antennae and wings. Fold one semi-circle in and then another one, so that it overlaps the first. The four semi-circles interlock to close the card. Tuck the last one carefully under the first fold so each fold holds the others in place.

5. Tweak the wings into place.

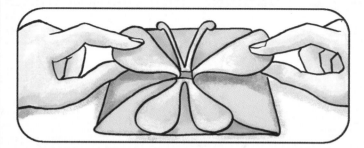

6. Now open the card carefully and write your message on the inside. Then fold it shut and colour in the butterfly's wings. Why not use a fine-tipped black pen to darken the antennae and draw on some pretty butterfly markings?

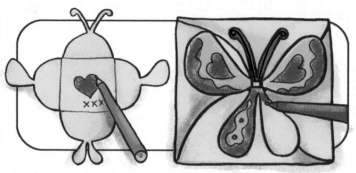

You can be as creative as you like with these cards. Try changing the shape of your template and using different colours and details to vary the look.

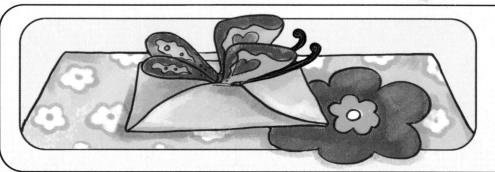

## TOP TIP

A flutterby butterfly card looks great as a gift tag. Simply stick it on with some folded-over sticky tape. Why not add a colourful paper flower?

# Good Hair Days

*Have you always wanted to try a new look? It doesn't matter how long your hair is because you can always style it so that it looks great. Try out some of these cool styles.*

## SHORT HAIR

Short hair has never been more stylish and there's plenty you can do to add a touch of glamour to it.

## ZIGZAG PARTING

Stand out from the crowd with a zigzag parting. It looks great and will also add volume to fine hair.

**1.** First, use the tip of a comb handle to create a straight parting.

**2.** Then, with the corner of the comb, draw a zigzag line from your forehead to the back of your head. Keep the line quite well spaced to start with.

**3.** Carefully comb the hair down each side to reveal a neat, zigzag parting.

**4.** Use some hairspray, or light mousse to secure the style in place.

Your zigzag parting will instantly transform your hair style and give it plenty of body and bounce.

Try to avoid running your hands through your hair because you will lose the zigzag pattern!

# I DIDN'T KNOW THAT!

Throughout history hair styles have changed a lot, but the art of hairdressing only developed during the reign of King Louis XV of France, in the 18th century. Louis liked to host elaborate fancy dress parties in the royal court. Young women tried to look their very best. They hired artists to create extravagant new hairstyles for them. Some girls even wore live birds in cages, waterfalls, toy ships recreating famous battle scenes or figures of cupids in their hair! The artists became highly skilled at their work and by 1767 there were over 1,200 hair artists or hairdressers in Paris. Unfortunately the fancy hairstyles often became infested with lice, so it wasn't long before wigs became fashionable instead.

# SHOULDER-LENGTH HAIR

There are lots of ways to wear your hair if it's a medium length, whether it's curly, or straight.

## POODLE BUNCHES

This cool style is lively and full of movement, and guaranteed to get you noticed.
1. Use the tip of a comb handle to create a neat, centre parting.

2. Take the hair on one side of your parting and pop it into a scrunchie to keep it out of the way.
3. Brush the other side down. Then lift the hair by brushing from underneath and draw it into a really high bunch above your ear.

4. Once you have the hair neatly arranged in a high bunch, secure it with a covered band (these are kinder to your hair).

5. Using the same technique set the other half of your hair in a high bunch (make sure they are secured at the same height). Add long ribbons into the bunches.

6. Alternatively you could twist each of your high bunches and secure them with another band.

# MEDIUM TO LONG HAIR

Up or down, long hair can be worn in many different ways.

## SLEEK SIDE PONYTAIL

This style is sleek and stylish and it's really easy to do.
1. Comb any tangles out.
2. Bring all the hair to one side and brush it down smoothly.

3. Secure it with a small band at the side of your head.
4. Loosen a length of hair from the ponytail and wrap it around the band to cover it.

5. Secure the ponytail with a clip to add a touch of glamour. Finally, use some light mousse, or gel, to give it a really sleek, tidy finish.

# DOUBLE PONYTAIL

This is great if you have thick hair, or if you're growing out a fringe.

**1.** Before you start, brush your hair well.

**2.** Create a sideways parting across the back of your head, above your ears, with the comb.

**3.** Draw the top section of hair into a ponytail and secure with a hairband.

**4.** Brush the lower section of hair and draw into a lower ponytail with a hairband.

**5.** Add a pretty hairclip to the top ponytail for a touch of glamour.

**6.** Finally, try teasing out a few locks of hair to frame your face. This will soften the style and add a hint of laid-back chic.

There are lots of different ways you can style your hair, whatever type and length it is. Try these...

# Sugar Pearls

*These sweets are great for parties, or for giving as a gift to a friend.*
*Plus they're quick and easy to make, so why not have a go!*

**You will need:** 225 g icing sugar / 1 egg white / peppermint essence / red food colouring.

**1.** Sift the icing sugar into a bowl.

**2.** Take another bowl. Use an electric hand whisk to lightly whip the egg white for a few seconds.

**3.** Add a heaped spoonful of the icing sugar to the egg white, using a wooden spoon, and beat for another 5 minutes.

**4.** Add the essence and the rest of the icing sugar to the bowl, bit by bit, and beat or whisk until fluffy peaks are formed. Add more sugar if the mixture looks runny.

**5.** Now add a few small drops of red food colouring and stir. Don't mix it in thoroughly, so you create a marble effect.

**6.** Dust a chopping board with icing sugar and roll out the mixture using a rolling pin, then shape into small circles.

Leave the sweets to dry out for 24 hours. Then store them in an airtight container. Yummy!

# Handy Pony Game

The Handy Pony challenge is the most keenly contested event at gymkhanas.
Prove your skills by playing this game with friends. All you need is a dice and some different
coloured counters. Take turns rolling the dice and moving on the number of spaces shown.

START

FINISH

Your foot's slipped out of the stirrup. Throw an even number to move on.

Your pony jumped the hay bale first time. Throw again.

Your pony refused a jump. Throw an odd number to continue.

Congratulations! You've won first prize.

Your hat has slipped forward. Miss a go while you put it straight.

You managed the 'open and close the gate' test in record time. Throw again.

Your pony knocked down three poles from a jump. Go back 3.

You catch a loose pony for a rider who fell off. Throw again.

You missed a cone in the slalom. Miss a go.

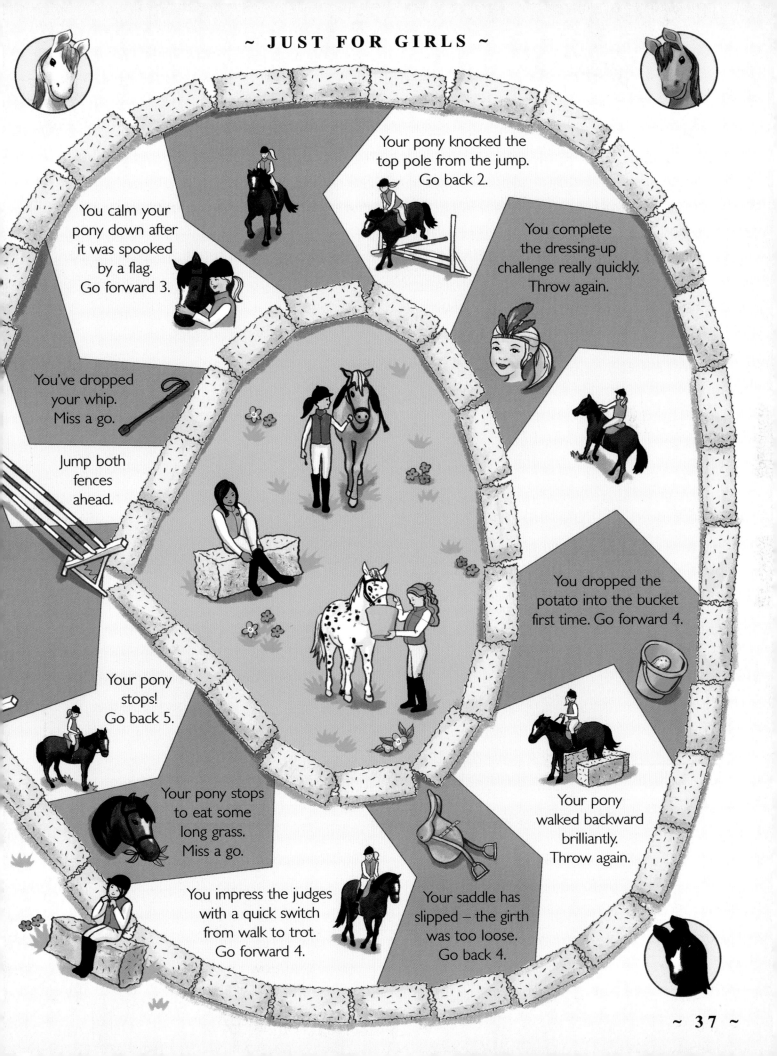

You calm your pony down after it was spooked by a flag. Go forward 3.

Your pony knocked the top pole from the jump. Go back 2.

You complete the dressing-up challenge really quickly. Throw again.

You've dropped your whip. Miss a go.

Jump both fences ahead.

You dropped the potato into the bucket first time. Go forward 4.

Your pony stops! Go back 5.

Your pony stops to eat some long grass. Miss a go.

You impress the judges with a quick switch from walk to trot. Go forward 4.

Your saddle has slipped – the girth was too loose. Go back 4.

Your pony walked backward brilliantly. Throw again.

# Give A Rosette

*Usually you would expect to win a rosette at a horse show. But did you know that they also make great gifts on special occasions? Next time, say 'Happy Birthday', 'Congratulations' or 'Thank You' in winning style.*

**You will need:** scissors / card / masking tape or sticky tape / coloured crêpe paper / glue / a safety pin or a kitchen tie.

1. Cut out a circle of card with the scissors, about 7 centimetres in diameter.

2. Cover the card with masking tape, wrapping it around and around, with the sticky side facing outward on both sides. This is the base of your rosette.

3. Take a strip of coloured crêpe paper, about 50 centimetres long and 5 centimetres wide. Press one end of it on to one side of the card. Start folding it into lots of little pleats, and work your way all around the circle of card, as shown. Make sure you start and finish with a fold in the crêpe paper. This is the front of your rosette.

4. Trim off any extra paper. Tuck the final fold under the first to hide the join. Stick it in place with a small piece of sticky tape.

5. Cut out another circle of card, 7 centimetres in diameter. Glue it onto the back of your rosette.

6. Now take two strips of crêpe paper, about 20 centimetres long and 3 centimetres wide. Cut each of the ends into two points and tape them to the back of the rosette to form 'tails'.

7. Cut out a final circle of card, 5 centimetres in diameter and stick it in the middle of the front of the rosette, on top of the pleated paper. Write your message, such as 'First Prize', on it.

8. Tape the non-opening side of a safety pin to the back of the rosette, so you can pin it to your clothing. To hang it up, twist a kitchen tie into a loop and tape that to the back instead.

## ADD VARIETY

- Try using two strips of different coloured crêpe paper and attach in two layers around the card circle for a fuller, fancier effect.
- Try using ribbon instead of crêpe paper. You might need a stapler to help keep the pleats in place. Keep the staples in the centre so that you can cover them up with the smaller piece of card.
- Cover the central circle of card with gold or silver foil, and 'score' a message into it using a pencil tip.

# Pony Puzzlers

*So, you think you know all about horses. Why not test your knowledge against your friends' in this quiz? Answer 'true' or 'false' to the following questions. You could present a rosette to the person who gets the top score. All the answers are on page 61.*

1. A 'bit' stops the saddle from slipping.
2. A wide white stripe down the middle of a horse's face is called a 'star'.
3. Horses have small stomachs that can't handle large amounts of food at once. This is why they need to eat small amounts but frequently.
4. A yearling is a young horse less than one year old.

5. A palomino is a golden-coloured horse with a white mane and tail.
6. A female horse is called a 'doe'.
7. People measure the height of a pony in 'fingers'.
8. A good way to remove dried mud from a pony's coat is to use a rubber curry comb.
9. The 'shire' is the oldest known breed of horse.

10. The Spanish Riding School is in Vienna, Austria.
11. A 'hinny' is a cross between a female donkey and a male horse.
12. The term 'dressage' means grooming.

13. Horses and ponies have special bones in their knees.
14. A horse with a red ribbon in its tail means that it kicks.
15. Horses' hooves keep growing, like fingernails, and need trimming every few weeks.
16. Until a horse is five years' old you can tell its age just by counting how many teeth it has.
17. A 'farrier' looks after horses on a farm.
18. The wooden poles set on the ground and used to train horses are known as 'cavatappi'.

19. Horses' feet need cleaning with a hoof pick to avoid infection.
20. The Arab is the biggest breed of horse.

21. It's common for twin horses to live long lives.
22. Foxgloves are poisonous to horses.
23. The barrel, dock and stifle are all parts of a horse.
24. Anna Sewell wrote a famous novel about a horse called *Brown Beauty*.
25. There are about 50 different breeds of horses.

# Bag Bling

*Are you bored of carrying that same old boring bag every day?*
*Then why not jazz it up with a whole new look with these easy make-over tips?*

## SUPER-CUTE BAG PETS

Add a new look to your school bag by making some fluffy friends to watch over your pens and books.

**You will need:** a pencil / some paper / scissors / pins / fake fur / two googly eyes / fabric glue / thin strips of black felt or ribbon / pink felt.

**1.** Find a cartoon picture of a kitten (or your favourite animal) in a comic or a magazine or use the picture below.

**2.** Trace the shape of the animal onto some paper, then cut it out to make a template.
**3.** Pin the template to some fake fur and cut around it. Then remove the paper template. Don't throw it away – you may want to use it again.

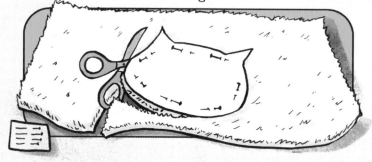

**4.** Now add some features. Start by attaching the googly eyes with the fabric glue.

**5.** Make some whiskers by cutting out six thin strips of black felt or ribbon. Stick three to each side of the face with fabric glue.
**6.** Make a nose from a small triangle cut from pink felt and glue it on.
**7.** Next, cut out a half-moon shape for the mouth. Why not add a semi-circle of pink felt for a tongue?

**8.** Add a ribbon tied in a bow for a pretty touch.
**9.** When the glue has dried, stick the animal face onto your school bag. Be careful to mop up any glue that seeps out at the edges.

Have a go making other animals, too – it's great fun!

# FLOWER POWER

Here's a great way to personalise your bag by giving it a splash of hippie chic. You start by making one big flower shape and then add lots more flowers, each getting smaller and smaller as they go towards the middle.

**You will need:** a pencil / a few sheets of coloured craft foam / scissors / PVA glue / a strip of self-adhesive hook-and-loop tape.

1. Draw a big flower shape onto the foam, about 10 centimetres across. You might find it easier to use the template shown here.
2. Next, draw smaller flower shapes of varying widths – 8, 6, 4 and 2 centimetres across. Try to use a different colour of foam for each one if you can. It works well if the smallest one is black or yellow. Cut out all the shapes.

3. You can now put the flower together – starting with the biggest shape at the bottom. Dab glue in the middle of each flower and stick the next one on to it. Keep going until all the shapes are stuck.

4. Now stick one stamp-sized square of hook-and-loop tape to the back of the flower and another to your bag and attach the flower.

5. For a great look, try making lots of different kinds of flowers in various colours. Then dot them all over your bag. That's serious flower power!

# DESIGNER DANGLES

Why not add some style by adding some designer dangles to your bag?

**You will need:** ribbons or shoe laces / beads.

Find some thin ribbons or shoe laces, in colours that look good with your bag. Fold one of them in half, making a loop at one end. Push the loop end through the hole in the zip-pull of your bag. Then thread the two loose ends through that loop. Tug the ends firmly to make a knot. Now thread a few beads onto each of the loose ends before tying a small knot at the bottom to hold them in place.

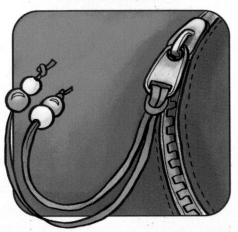

# Amnatra's Bracelet

*If you would like to have a special scarab bracelet similar to the one Amnatra wears on pages 42 – 45, then follow this guide to make one of your own.*

**You will need:** a packet of polymer clay* in either turquoise, purple or a deep blue colour / an old plate / a cocktail stick / a teaspoon / kitchen foil / clear nail varnish / turquoise poster paint / paper craft straws / a roll of silver or gold elastic thread.

\* Polymer clay is easy-to-use modelling clay — much less messy than real clay. It keeps its shape and sets hard after being baked for 15 to 20 minutes on a very low heat of 130°C/Gas Mark 0.5. You can buy it from most craft shops.

## STEP ONE: THE SCARABS

1. Take a little piece of clay (about the size of the top half of your thumb) and roll into a ball.
2. Using your fingertips, carefully shape the ball into an egg shape, so that it looks a bit like the shape of a beetle's body. To finish off the ball, smooth down its surfaces by gently rolling it around on a clean, flat surface, such as an old plate.
3. With the cocktail stick make a hole right through the clay egg. The hole should be big enough for several lengths of elastic thread to pass through it.

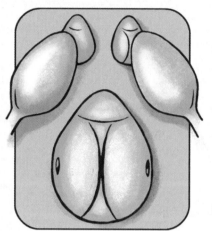

4. Press the tip of a teaspoon gently into the clay to make one curved line for the beetle's head and two for the wings, as shown (it's a little like the shape of a ladybird). When you have finished, make sure the hole through the egg is still intact.

5. Line a baking tray with kitchen foil and put your beetle on it. The foil will stop the clay from sticking to the tray.
6. Now make some more scarabs — maybe three or four — depending on the size of your wrist.
7. Bake the scarabs in the oven, following the instructions on the packet of the polymer clay.

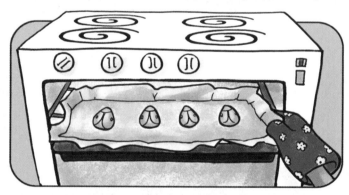

Don't worry if you over-bake the beetles and the clay goes black, you can paint over it once it has set.

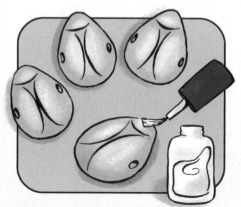

8. Leave the scarabs to cool and set hard. Then add some shine by painting them with nail varnish — clear nail varnish works well.

## STEP TWO: THE BEADS

1. Pour a little pool of turquoise poster paint into a saucer.
2. Snip lengths of paper straws (about 5 mm each) into the saucer and turn them over, so that they get fully coated with paint.

3. When the straws have nearly dried, lift them out and put on a piece of kitchen foil over a drying rack to dry completely.

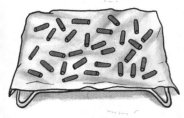

## STEP THREE: MAKE THE BRACELET

1. Cut three lengths of elastic thread that each measure about 50 centimetres long.
2. Tie the three lengths together, about 10 centimetres from one end, using a simple knot.

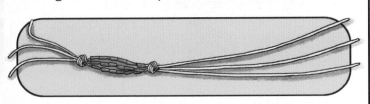

3. Now thread six of your turquoise beads along each strand of elastic. Make another knot next to the beads, to tie all three strands together. You are using the beads to space out the scarab beetles.

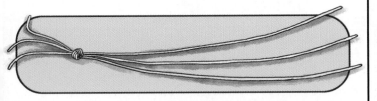

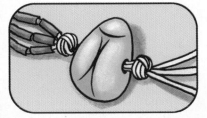

4. Take a scarab and thread all three strands of elastic through the hole and tie another knot.

5. Now thread six more beads along each strand of elastic and tie a knot.

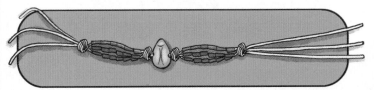

6. Take another scarab and thread it on, as before. Make another knot.

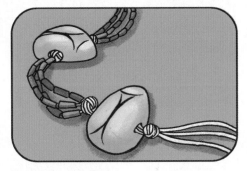

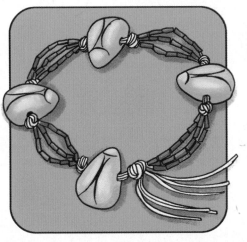

7. Keep repeating this process until you've got a length of bracelet that fits your wrist. Tie both ends together in a final knot, to complete the bracelet.

### • TOP TIP •

For funkier beads mix two colours of clay together until you get a marbled look.

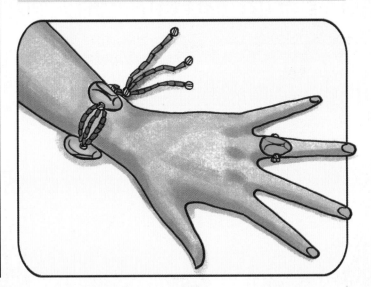

# Spooky Talon Salon

*What better time to get dressed up and try out weird and wonderful designs on your nails than Halloween. Put on some funky music, wear your scariest outfit and get spookily creative.*

Here are some nail decorating techniques to give you inspiration. Keep your finished nails looking good longer by adding a coat of clear varnish on top at the end.

You will need: false nails if your own are really short / assorted coloured nail varnish — including black, orange and red / cocktail sticks / a pen or pencil / paper / sticky-back plastic (masking tape works) / nail scissors / tweezers.

Organise your equipment by placing the polishes on one tray and everything else on another. Cover the table you are working on with newspaper and you're ready to go.

## GET BAT-TY

You can't have Halloween without some spooky bats flying around. This design uses a clever 'masking' technique to give a beautifully batty effect.

**1.** Draw the shape of a tiny bat onto the backing paper of some sticky-back plastic. Make sure the drawing is small enough to fit onto each of your fingernails.

**2.** Decide how many nails you want to decorate. It can take a while to cut out ten, so why not do every other finger? Use nail scissors to cut out the bat shapes, as they make it easier to cut around the wings.

**3.** Next, carefully paint all of your nails with the black nail varnish.

**4.** When your nails are completely dry, peel the bats from the backing paper. Press each shape into the middle of a nail.

**5.** Now paint over the bats and the whole nail of each finger using a different colour varnish. Red works really well.

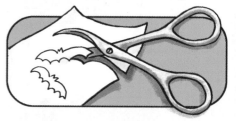

**6.** Once the varnish is dry, peel the bats off with some tweezers to reveal the black bats underneath.
**7.** Dip a cocktail stick into a different colour varnish and carefully dab tiny dots onto the bats' faces for eyes.

# SCARY PUMPKINS
Whooooah!

**1.** Paint each of your nails black and leave for a few minutes. (Use a set of false nails if your nails are too chewed!)

**2.** When your nails are completely dry, paint over each one, but this time with a bright orange coloured varnish.

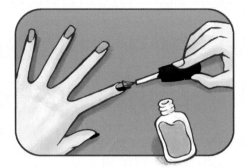

**3.** While the orange varnish is still sticky, use a cocktail stick to scrape a pumpkin face on each nail. Make sure you only scrape away the orange layer, to reveal the black varnish underneath. Start with two triangles for the eyes…

… and another one for the nose. Then add a jagged grin. Don't worry if you go wrong, you can just fill in the gaps with another small dab of orange varnish and go back to it in a couple of minutes.

**4.** Leave your nails to dry before showing all your friends. Try creating different pumpkin expressions on each of your nails.

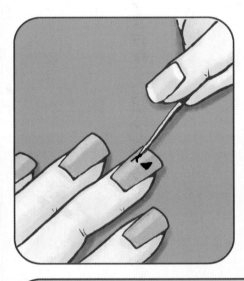

# SPOOKY SPIDERS
**1.** Paint a big blob of black nail varnish onto a finger nail. This will be a spider's body.
**2.** Use the tip of a cocktail stick to drag out eight legs from the wet varnish, four on either side.
**3.** Do the same thing on the rest of your nails.

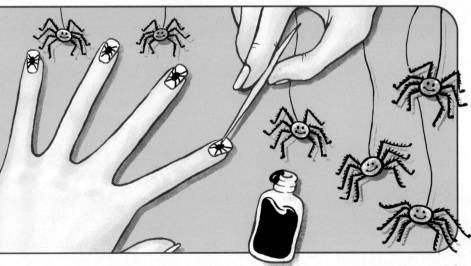

# Time to Dance

Who can resist the elegance and sparkle of the ballroom?
Look closely at the scene below.

# SPOT THE DIFFERENCE

Now see if you can spot 15 differences between these two dancing scenes.
Some of them are easier to find than others. Why not see if you can spot
more than your best friend?
You'll find the answers on page 61.

# Rainbow Moods

*The colours we choose to wear and surround ourselves with can affect the way we feel and the way people see us. Take a look at these pages and see how to make colours work for you.*

## HOW TO PICK THE RIGHT COLOURS

Designers use colours to create different moods. One useful way to choose a colour scheme is to use a colour wheel, like the one below.

To make a room feel lively and fun, choose rich, contrasting colours. Try shades that are opposite each other on the colour wheel, such as green and red.

If you want a room to look sophisticated, choose pale shades that appear two stages apart. A pale orange looks nice with a light purple.

To create a calming mood, try a combination of colours that are next to each other on the colour wheel – from the same 'family' – for instance, blue and green.

Remember to think about which direction your room faces. If the windows face south and lots of warm daylight comes in, then you can go for cooler shades such as pale blue. If the room faces north, then the light will be paler and it's better to choose warm shades of your favourite colours to brighten it up, such as a golden yellow, not a lemon yellow.

But what does your favourite colour mean and what does it say about you? Read on to find out.

## RED

Red can look welcoming and warm in large rooms and quite cosy in smaller spaces. But too much red can make a room feel angry or claustrophobic.

If you like red, you are probably lively, fun-loving, ambitious and bold. But you can also be a bit moody.

## WHITE

White is a peaceful, comforting colour. It can make a room look clean and smart, but too much of it can feel cold and bare.

If you love white, you enjoy a simple, easy-going life and are probably quite calm with high ideals.

## PURPLE

Purple can have a calming effect. It can make a room look sophisticated, imaginative and interesting.

If you're passionate about purple, you're sensitive and artistic with a great sense of humour and are drawn to friends who understand you.

# PINK

Pink is a calming colour and it can help you to sleep. Pale pink rooms make great chill-out pads, but bright pinks can give a room lots of energy.

If pink is your favourite colour, you're charming, sociable and talented. You're an incurable romantic and you enjoy the good things in life.

# GREEN

Green is said to be the colour of harmony and balance. It can make a room feel calm and restful.

If you like green, you're probably quite calm and fair-minded. You enjoy helping your friends because you're generous and kind. You also like to have hobbies and join clubs.

# ORANGE

A light shade of orange can have a gently warming effect on a room. Brighter shades look quite exciting and can make people feel like talking.

If orange is your favourite colour, you're fun-loving and popular, plus you love being the centre of attention. You also have a sense of curiosity, but get bored quite easily.

# BLUE

Blue is the colour of truth and harmony and it makes a room feel calming and cool. Pale shades can bring a feeling of wellbeing.

If you love blue, you're cool, brave and confident. But you also have a strong sense of responsibility, so be careful about taking risks.

# YELLOW

Yellow is associated with happiness and wisdom. It can make a room feel warm and cheerful, but a bright shade can make some people feel anxious.

If yellow is your chosen colour, you'll have a sunny personality and a fun sense of humour. You probably enjoy exploring and you seek out adventure.

# BLACK

Black is a sophisticated and dramatic colour. In small amounts it can look bold and elegant and works well as a contrast to other colours.

If you like black, you probably have contrasting elements in your personality. You might be quite serious and grown-up, but you also have secret wishes and deep emotions.

# Jazzed-up Junk

*Want to breathe new life into those trinkets that have been lying around and brighten up your bedroom at the same time? Then follow these simple ideas that won't cost you a thing!*

## COMFY CUDDLE-CUSHION

These cushions are a great way to recycle your old clothes and accessorise your room at the same time.

**You will need:** an old woollen jumper / a cushion / pins / scissors / fabric glue / self-adhesive hook-and-loop tape.

1. Take the jumper and put it through a really hot wash in the washing machine to shrink the fibres a little – that way the stitches won't come undone as easily. When it is dry, lay it out flat on a table.

2. Check that your cushion is the right size, by placing the cushion inside the jumper. It should fit tightly across the width – if not, you will need a different sized cushion.

3. Remove the cushion and turn the jumper inside out.
4. Pin a line across the jumper, just below the arm holes. Then take the scissors and cut above your line. You should now have a square or rectangular, woollen tube.

5. The bottom hem of the jumper has a 'finished edge'. Start here and glue one side of a strip of hook and loop tape along about a centimetre from the finished edge. Then turn the woolly tube over and stick the other side of the strip.

6. Now fold over the top edge of the tube about 2 centimetres. Stick this down with fabric glue. Place some heavy books on top and leave to set for a few hours.

7. When the glue has dried, stick on a strip of hook and loop tape along both sides of the top edge.

8. Turn your cover the right way round and insert the cushion. Press the hook and loop strips together to secure and you're done!

# MIRROR, MIRROR ON THE WALL

Why not jazz up an old mirror by adding interesting shapes and textures to the frame?

**You will need:** an old mirror – go for one with a flat frame, so that it's easier to stick things to it / newspaper / masking tape / sandpaper / a selection of any or all of the following – beads, broken necklaces, sea shells, small pebbles, pasta shapes, pistachio shells and paper clips / PVA glue / an old paintbrush / paint.

1. Before you start, protect the glass area of the mirror with some newspaper, stuck down with pieces of masking tape.

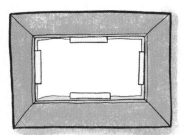

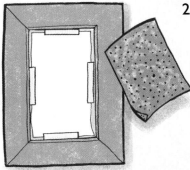

2. Cover a table with newspaper and lay the mirror on it, facing upward. Gently rub the frame with sandpaper to roughen the surface a little – this will help things stick to it.

3. Take your collection of trinkets and start placing them onto the frame. Try setting out different arrangements until you're completely happy. You might decide to go for a design that mixes up all of the objects…

…or have sections for each item, divided by pieces of string or rows of beads…

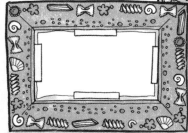

…or how about a border of large shapes, with smaller ones inside?

4. When you're happy with your design, remove the objects from one section of the frame and squirt some glue onto the frame in small blobs, or paint it on with a small brush. Then take the objects, one-by-one, and add a little blob of glue to the back of each before you stick it on.

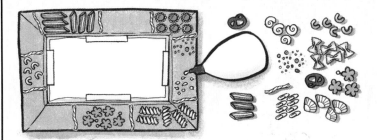

Repeat with the other sections until the frame is completely covered. Then leave overnight for the glue to dry completely.

5. Now you can paint the frame and trinkets, making sure that the paint gets into every last spot. Be careful not to knock off any of the objects. If you do, you can just paint the object and glue it back on once you've finished painting the rest of the frame. Finally, dilute some PVA glue in an equal amount of water and paint it over everything on the frame, to protect it.

# A MAGAZINE TIDY

Are you forever losing things under piles of magazines in your bedroom? Then why not make yourself a cool set of storage boxes, to keep your room tidy and add some sparkle at the same time?

**You will need:** scissors / three cereal boxes big enough to hold your favourite magazine / a pencil / a ruler / PVA glue / kitchen towel or newspaper / masking tape / paint / glitter paint / plain paper.

1. Carefully trim the top off each cereal box.

2. Take one and draw a line across the width of one of the narrow sides, about 12 centimetres from the bottom. Mark a point along the top edge, about 10 centimetres along from the opposite narrow side.

3. Use a ruler to draw two diagonal lines on the front and back of the box, to connect the two points, as shown.
4. Cut along the three marked lines.

5. Do the same for the other two boxes. Then put some newspaper down and cover the outside of each box in a thick layer of PVA glue. The easiest way is to rest the boxes upside down over a plastic jug, or squash bottle. Rip up small pieces of kitchen towel (or newspaper) and press them into the glue, so that they overlap slightly.

Repeat this process two or three times to strengthen the boxes. Don't worry if some of the pieces stick over the edge – you can trim them once the glue has dried.

6. When the boxes are dry, stick strips of masking tape along each of the edges, to neaten them. You're going to paint over this later, so it won't be seen.

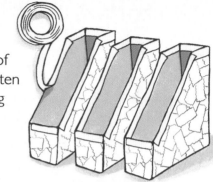

7. Now you can choose your colour scheme. Be daring! Think of bright, contrasting colours – perhaps red and black, or something trendy like pale blue and chocolate brown.

8. Now paint each box in your chosen colour, using a medium-sized brush. It might take a couple of coats to get a good covering. Vinyl or emulsion paint will work better than gloss (DIY shops will have tester pots you can buy cheaply). Again, the best way is to put the box upside down over a bottle, so you can paint it all in one go. If you like, you can paint the inside of the boxes, but you don't have to because they will face the wall.

9. When the paint is dry, turn the boxes the right-way up and arrange them in a row.

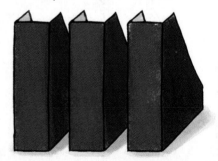

10. Draw a large flower and stem on a sheet of plain paper. Make it big enough to cover all three boxes, side on. Use the template on the next page, if you like. Then turn the paper over and paint the other side in your contrast colour.

Draw a line on the shape to mark where the box edges are, then cut the flower into sections and glue them on. The flower will look complete when the boxes are lined up.

13. Now give your desk tidies a protective glaze. Once the flower is stuck, dilute some PVA glue in an equal amount of water and paint it over the boxes, especially over the flower.

14. Finally, add some sparkle by brushing on some glitter paint. Then line them up on your desk, with the flower facing outward – simple!

11. When the paint is dry, you should still be able to see your outline. Cut out the flower shape – this way, your edges should look really neat.
12. Line up the boxes and choose where you want the flower to go – maybe in one corner, rather than in the middle.

# Furry Friends

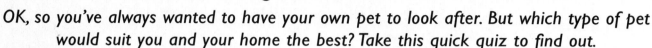

*OK, so you've always wanted to have your own pet to look after. But which type of pet would suit you and your home the best? Take this quick quiz to find out.*

1. How much time do you think you could spare each day to look after your pet?
   (a) five minutes
   (b) one hour
   (c) half an hour
   (d) quarter of an hour.

2. How much outdoor space have you got?
   (a) no garden
   (b) a large garden
   (c) a small lawn
   (d) a paved patio.

3. How many children live in your house?
   (a) just you
   (b) two or more brothers and sisters, all ages
   (c) one younger brother, or sister
   (d) one older brother, or sister.

4. Which of these do you live in?
   (a) a city
   (b) a town
   (c) a farm
   (d) a village.

5. Your neighbour asks you to look after his pet mouse while he goes away on holiday. Do you…
   (a) check with your parents before you agree and then make sure you know what to do
   (b) say 'no – I hate mice!'
   (c) say 'yes' and take it home right away
   (d) say you're not sure how to, so you need to find out more before you decide.

6. How much experience do you have looking after animals?
   (a) some
   (b) a lot
   (c) very little
   (d) none.

7. A kitten shows you a cool new trick. Do you…
   (a) give it some tuna chunks
   (b) teach it a new trick
   (c) feed it some cream
   (d) give it a big cuddle.

8. Your male guinea pig looks lonely. Do you…
   (a) buy him a male companion
   (b) buy him a female companion
   (c) buy him a wheel
   (d) shrug – how can you tell? It's a guinea pig.

**9.** On bonfire night, your friend says she wants to bring her puppy to your firework party. Do you…
(a) agree – all dogs love parties
(b) suggest she stays home to make sure it's safe
(c) say she can bring it, if it's left in the car
(d) tell her to tie it up in the garage, to stop it running away.

**10.** A neighbour invites you to come and see her new rabbits. Do you…
(a) invite three friends to go with you
(b) go on your own and take a carrot
(c) go along and let the rabbits out onto the veggie patch for fun
(d) take your best friend with you.

**11.** It's raining, but you've been asked to finish cleaning the rabbit hutch in the garden. Do you…
(a) ask if you can wait until the rain stops
(b) try to get out of it – it can wait
(c) put on some wellies and get the job done
(d) finish cleaning the hutch, but reluctantly.

**12.** It's the weekend before a big test at school and you feel nervous. Do you…
(a) watch TV with a mug of hot chocolate
(b) lie on the sofa and read a book
(c) relax in a warm bubble-bath
(d) go running in the park to unwind.

**13.** Your friend treads mud through your bedroom by mistake. Do you…
(a) clean it up yourself
(b) ask your friend to clean it up
(c) ignore it
(d) tell an adult and let them clean it up.

**14.** Your friend looks pale in class. Do you…
(a) tell her to pull herself together
(b) take her to see the school nurse
(c) give her some chocolate
(d) sympathise.

**15.** You are asked to help at an after-school club for children of different ages. Do you…
(a) say 'no thanks, I'm busy'
(b) find a box of dolls and have a pretend picnic
(c) organise some team games outside
(d) hand out sweets and leave them to it.

Now work out your score, then turn to page 61 to see what pet would suit you.

| | a | b | c | d |
|---|---|---|---|---|
| **1.** | a = 1 | b = 4 | c = 3 | d = 2 |
| **2.** | a = 1 | b = 4 | c = 3 | d = 2 |
| **3.** | a = 4 | b = 1 | c = 2 | d = 3 |
| **4.** | a = 1 | b = 2 | c = 4 | d = 3 |
| **5.** | a = 4 | b = 1 | c = 2 | d = 3 |
| **6.** | a = 3 | b = 4 | c = 2 | d = 1 |
| **7.** | a = 2 | b = 3 | c = 1 | d = 4 |
| **8.** | a = 4 | b = 2 | c = 3 | d = 1 |
| **9.** | a = 1 | b = 4 | c = 3 | d = 2 |
| **10.** | a = 2 | b = 4 | c = 1 | d = 3 |
| **11.** | a = 2 | b = 1 | c = 4 | d = 3 |
| **12.** | a = 1 | b = 3 | c = 2 | d = 4 |
| **13.** | a = 4 | b = 3 | c = 1 | d = 2 |
| **14.** | a = 1 | b = 4 | c = 2 | d = 3 |
| **15.** | a = 1 | b = 3 | c = 4 | d = 2 |

# Answers

## It's A Girls' World: page 9
### WHERE IN THE WORLD?
1. c   2. c   3. c   4. a   5. b   6. a
7. b   8. a   9. c   10. a   11. b

## Catwalk Capers: pages 20-21
### ON YOUR TOES
There are 10 pairs altogether.

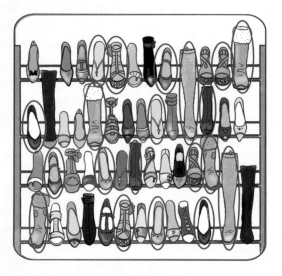

### MAKE-UP FIX

### ALL TANGLED UP
**A** = 1 **B** = 3 **C** = 4 **D** = 2

### PHOTO MANIA
1 = D 2 = B 3 = E 4 = C 5 = A

## Ocean Centre: pages 28-29
### SPOT THE SEAHORSE
There are 20 seahorses lurking in the tank.

### SEEING DOUBLE
Angelfishes D and I are identical.

### WHICH WAY IS HOME?

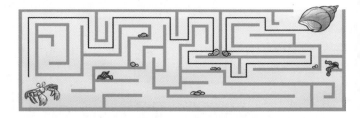

### DOLPHIN DILEMMA

### SEABED SEARCH
There are 19 starfish and 17 sea urchins in the tank.

### TURTLE MIX
Boxes B, C, D and G appear in the main picture.

# Pony Puzzlers: page 39

1. False. You use the 'girth'. 2. False. It's a 'blaze'. 3. True. 4. False. It's between one and two years old. 5. True. 6. False. It's a 'mare'. 7. False. Height is measured in 'hands': one hand equals 16 cm. 8. True. 9. False. It's the biggest. The Arabian is the oldest. 10. True. 11. True. 12. False. Dressage is a type of horse training with competitions. 13. True. 14. True. 15. True. 16. True. After five years they just grow longer. 17. False. A 'farrier' looks after a horse's hooves. 18. False. The poles are actually called 'cavalletti'. Cavatappi is macaroni. 19. True. 20. False. It's the oldest. The shire is the biggest. 21. False. Many vets say that a horse is not designed to successfully carry twins through pregnancy, and often one of the twin horse foals dies before birth. 22. True. 23. True. 24. False. She wrote the novel *Black Beauty*. 25. False. There are over 100 different breeds of horses in the world.

**0–9 questions right:** You're still a novice, but there's plenty of time yet! Third prize.

**10–18 questions right:** Pretty good. You're a great fan, so why not find out more? Second prize.

**19–25 questions right:** You really know your stuff – red rosette for first prize and lap of honour to you.

# Time To Dance: pages 50-51

# Perfect Pets: pages 58-59

**0–15 points:** Some pets such as hamsters and gerbils don't need a garden, but if you don't have much time to spare, then perhaps pets aren't for you. Even a goldfish needs to be fed regularly, and their tank cleaned and water refreshed. The thought of being responsible for another creature simply doesn't appeal. You'd be better off watching a wild life programme on television than actually having a pet.

**16–30 points:** You will probably enjoy smaller pets that are easier to manage. If you've got younger siblings, then guinea pigs are great, being calm and easy to pick up. Don't mix males and females, though, or you'll end up with more than you want! You think animals are great fun, but maybe you need more experience in learning how to look after them and seeing to their needs. You like your comforts, so choose a pet to fit in with your lifestyle.

**31–45 points:** A small dog would be fine, if you have the room, as would rabbits, guinea pigs, gerbils, hamsters and white mice. You realise that smaller animals need quiet, careful handling and you know that everyone must be very careful not to let them escape! You're kind and considerate to animals, and love to have them around. Small, cute animals are definitely your thing – the fluffier the better!

**46–60 points:** If you have a big garden and plenty of space, you can manage lots of different sizes, from tiny mice to large dogs. The bigger the animal, the more you need to exercise it – make sure you can handle the responsibility. You'll enjoy playing with a dog, for instance, but you'll be keen to train it, so it will be happy and safe. You'll be a great owner, particularly of a new puppy, or a rescue dog from a shelter, who'll needs lots of love.